Chri

B i b l e S t u d i e s

MW01225566

PURSUING HOLINESS

Carolyn Nystrom

in 6 or 12 studies
for individuals or groups

With Notes for Leaders

INTERVARSITY PRESS
DOWNERS GROVE, ILLINOIS 60515

InterVarsity Press is the book-publishing division of InterVarsity Christian Fellowship, a student movement active on campus at hundreds of universities, colleges and schools of nursing in the United States of America, and a member movement of the International Fellowship of Evangelical Students. For information about local and regional activities, write Public Relations Dept., InterVarsity Christian Fellowship, 6400 Schroeder Rd., P.O. Box 7895, Madison, WI 53707-7895.

All Scripture quotations, unless otherwise indicated, are taken from the HOLY BIBLE, NEW INTERNATIONAL VERSION. Copyright © 1973, 1978, 1984 International Bible Society. Used by permission of Zondervan Publishing House. All rights reserved.

Cover photograph: Robert McKendrick

ISBN 0-8308-1147-8

Printed in the United States of America ∞

15	14	13	12	11	10	9	8	7	6	5	4
03	02	01	00	99	98	97	96	95			

Contents

Welcome to Christian Character Bible Studies

What is a Christian character? And how does one go about developing it?

As with most questions of faith and the practice of faith, the best source of information is the Bible itself. The Christian Character Bible Studies explore a wide variety of biblical passages that speak of character development.

The Bible speaks of love—love for ourselves, love for God, love for other believers, and love for those who do not yet believe.

The Bible speaks of responsibility—responsibility for the poor, responsibility for the weak, responsibility for the environment, responsibility for our assets, responsibility to work and responsibility to share our faith.

The Bible speaks of holy living—honesty, sexual purity, mental discipline, faithfulness, courage and obedience.

The Bible speaks of hope—a hope that is based on the character of God, the work of Jesus Christ, and an accurate view of our human limitations. It is a hope that says, "Residence on earth is temporary; residence in heaven is eternal."

This series of Bible study guides will help you explore, in

thought and in practice, these many facets of Christian character. But why bother? Why can't we accept ourselves the way we are? Isn't that the route to mental health?

Not entirely. We are all in transition. Each new day brings new influences on who we are. We respond—and change. With God's help, that change can be toward Christian growth.

Growing in character is satisfying. It carries with it the sense of growing in godliness—into the image that God created us to be. It carries a sense of harmony, of walking hand in hand with God. But it is not painless. Therefore these guides will constantly ask us to hold up our character to the mirror of Scripture and to bend that character along the lines of Christ's image. God doesn't want us to stay the same. We should allow the Spirit to nudge us through these studies toward the spiritual maturity that God designed for his people.

What Kind of Guide Is This?
This is an inductive Bible study guide. That means that each study deals with a particular passage of Scripture and attempts to understand its content, its meaning, and its implications for godly living. A variety of questions will explore all three of those areas.

This is a thought-provoking guide. Each question assumes a variety of answers. Many questions do not have "right" answers, particularly questions that aim at meaning or application. Instead, the questions should inspire users to explore the passage in more depth.

This study guide is flexible—you can use it for individual study or in a group. You can vary the amount of time you take for each study, and you have various options for the number of studies you do from the guide. This is possible because every guide in this series is structured with two unique features. First, each of the six studies is divided into two parts, and second, several questions are marked with an asterisk (*), indicating that they may be

Guidelines for Using the Christian Character Bible Studies

Option	Type of Use	Time Allowed	Number of Sessions	Your Plan to Follow
1	Individual	30 minutes	12	Divide each study into two sessions, and use all the questions.
2	Individual	45 minutes	6	Use one study per session, and skip questions with an asterisk (*) if time doesn't allow for them.
3	Individual	60 minutes	6	Use one study per session, and use all the questions.
4	Group	30 minutes	12	Divide each study into two sessions, and skip questions with an asterisk(*) if time doesn't allow for them.
5	Group	45-60 minutes	12	Divide each study into two sessions, and use all the questions.
6	Group	60 minutes	6	Use one study per session, and skip questions with an asterisk (*) if time doesn't allow for them.
7	Group	90 minutes	6	Use one study per session, and use all the questions.

skipped if time does not allow for them. So you can have six sessions or twelve, with varying amounts of time to fit your needs.

How do you decide which approach is best for you? Looking at the chart on page 6, decide if you will be using this guide for individual study or in a group. Then determine how much time you want to spend on each session and how many sessions you want to have. Then follow the plan described in the far right column.

For example, if you are using this guide in a group, you can choose from options 4, 5, 6 or 7. If you have 45-60 minutes for study and discussion in each group meeting, then you can use option 5. Or if you have only 30 minutes available, you can use option 4. These options allow you to have twelve meetings by breaking at the dividing point in each session and using all the questions, including those with an asterisk.

If your group has only six meeting times available, then follow the column headed "Number of Sessions" down to options 6 and 7. Option 6 provides for 60-minute sessions without the asterisked questions while option 6 allows for 90-minute sessions using all the questions.

Note that there are four plans that allow for in-depth study—options 1, 3, 5 and 7. These use each of the questions and will allow for the most thorough examination of Scripture and of ourselves.

With seven different options available to you, Christian Character Bible Studies offer maximum flexibility to suit your schedule and needs.

Each study is composed of three sections: an introduction with a question of approach to the topic of the day, questions that invite study of the passage or passages, and leader's notes at the back of the book. The section of questions provides space for writing observations, either in preparation for the study or during the course of the discussion. This space can form a permanent record of your thoughts and spiritual progress.

Suggestions for Individual Study

1. Read the introduction. Consider the opening question, and make notes about your responses to it.

2. Pray, asking God to speak to you from his Word about this particular topic.

3. Read the passage in a modern translation of the Bible, marking phrases that seem important. Note in the margin any questions that come to your mind as you read.

4. Use the questions from the study guide to more thoroughly examine the passage. (Questions are phrased from the New International Version of the Bible.) Note your findings in the space provided. After you have made your own notes, read the corresponding leader's notes in the back of the book for further insights. (You can ignore the comments about moderating the dynamics of a discussion group.) Consult the bibliography for further information.

5. Re-read the entire passage, making further notes about its general principles and about the personal use you intend to make of them.

6. Pray. Speak to God about insights you have gained into his character—and your own. Tell him of any desires you have for specific growth. Ask his help as you attempt to live out the principles described in that passage.

Suggestions for Group Study

Joining a Bible study group can be a great avenue to spiritual growth. Here are a few guidelines that will help you as you participate in the studies in this guide.

1. These are inductive Bible studies. That means that you will discuss a particular passage of Scripture—in-depth. Only rarely should you refer to other portions of the Bible, and then only at the request of the leader. Of course, the Bible is internally consistent, and other good forms of study draw on that consistency, but inductive Bible

study sticks with a single passage and works on it in-depth.

2. These are discussion studies. Questions in this guide aim at helping a group discuss together a passage of Scripture in order to understand its content, meaning and implications. Most people are either natural talkers or natural listeners. Yet this type of study works best if people participate more or less evenly. Try to curb any natural tendency to either excessive talking or excessive quiet. You and the rest of the group will benefit.

3. Most questions in this guide invite a variety of answers. If you disagree with someone else's comment, say so (kindly). Then explain your own point-of-view from the passage before you.

4. Be willing to lead a discussion. Much of the preparation for leading has already been accomplished in the writing of this guide. If you have observed someone else direct the discussion two or three times, you are probably ready to lead.

5. Respect the privacy of others in your group. Many people speak of things within the context of a Bible study/prayer group, that they do not want as public knowledge. Assume that personal information spoken within the group setting is private, unless you are specifically told otherwise. And don't talk about it elsewhere.

6. Enjoy your study. Prepare to grow. God bless.

Suggestions for Group Leaders

Specific suggestions to help you appear in the leader's notes at the back of this guide. Read the opening section of the leader's notes carefully, even if you are only leading one group meeting. Then you can go to the section on the particular study you will lead.

Introducing Pursuing Holiness

"But just as he who called you is holy, so be holy in all you do; for it is written: 'Be holy, because I am holy.' "

This startling command is tucked midway through First Peter, chapter 1. If a monk of the Middle Ages had quoted this passage to fellow monks who lived in a high craggy monastery, full of midnight prayer and morning song, far above the grit of pickpockets and feuding landholders, we might say, "Yes, a lofty goal, but it fits the setting and the people. Perhaps, with lifelong effort, they can do it."

But these words came from Peter, a sweaty ex-fisherman. Even his language speaks of hard work and meager education.

It was Peter who first refused to let Christ wash his feet, then demanded a full bath. It was Peter who said he would die before he abandoned Christ, then within twelve hours swore three times that he'd never met the man. It was Peter who threw himself overboard in a storm so that he could meet Jesus walking toward him, then had to be rescued from the waves like any ordinary drowning man. And his readers were no more likely recipients of such a command than the writer was to give it.

Peter addressed his letter to "God's elect, strangers in the world," then he listed geographic locations throughout the then-known universe. His readers had been flung there, no doubt, by the Jerusalem dispersion, an enforced relocation of Christian believers because of religious tensions with devout Jews.

As if the pressures of maintaining an "odd" faith in a foreign environment were not enough, Peter went on to promise his readers that they must prepare for intense persecution. Nero was on the throne, and the kindly five years when Nero's mother, Agrippina, ruled from behind the throne, were over. Nero's madness was becoming more apparent. Soon half of Rome would burn (perhaps at

Nero's own hand) and Nero, needing a scapegoat, would choose Christians. Bearing the name of Christ could then send a believer to the sports arena, covered with animal fur, as a bait for hungry beasts. Or it could impale him on a jagged pole as a human torch for one of Nero's midnight picnics.

Still Peter urged holiness, commanded it—because God is holy. Seeking holiness may not earn today's Christian a participant's ticket to the arena, but it is hardly a popular pursuit. We are a breed of blenders, of diplomats, of context evangelists. We don't like to be set apart, different. Holiness smacks of prudishness, and judgmentalism, and rigid codes of conduct. We visualize tight-lipped women and ogre-jowled men with low tolerance and big sticks.

But such images do not fit early teachers of holiness, nor do they measure God.

John Wesley, founder of the Methodist denomination and one who helped define modern-day holiness, saw holiness as an act of love both to God and to people. In 1739, he wrote:

A Methodist is one who loves the Lord his God with all his heart, with all his soul, with all his mind, and with all his strength. God is the joy of his heart and the desire of his soul is continually crying out. Whom have I in Heaven but you; and there is none upon earth whom I desire besides you. My God and my all! You are the strength of my heart, and my portion forever. He is therefore happy in God, yea always happy, as having in him a well of water spring up into everlasting life, and overflowing his soul with peace and joy. . . .

And loving God, he loves his neighbor as himself; he loves every man as his own soul. He loves his enemies, yea, and the enemies of God. And if it be not in his power to do good to them that hate him, yet he ceases not to pray for them, tho' they spurn his love, and still despitefully use him and persecute him.

Indeed joy and love fill the Wesley hymns, as in this song from 1738.

O grant that nothing in my soul

> May dwell, but thy pure love alone!
> O may thy love possess me whole,
>   My joy, my treasure, and my crown;
> Strange fires far from my heart remove:
> My every, act, word, thought, be love![1]

When the Old Testament prophet Isaiah glimpsed a holy God, he colored (for us) a picture of God's majesty and glory.

"In the year that King Uzziah died, I saw the Lord seated on a throne, high and exalted, and the train of his robe filled the temple. Above him were seraphs, each with six wings: With two wings they covered their faces, with two they covered their feet, and with two they were flying. And they were calling to one another:

> 'Holy, holy, holy is the LORD Almighty;
>   the whole earth is full of his glory.'

At the sound of their voices the doorposts and thresholds shook and the temple was filled with smoke.

'Woe to me!' I cried. 'I am ruined! For I am a man of unclean lips, and I live among a people of unclean lips, and my eyes have seen the King, the LORD Almighty." (Isaiah 6:1-5)

John Wesley's view of holiness inspired love and joy. Isaiah's glimpse of a holy God inspired awe and worship—and a need for cleansing. This study guide is an attempt to capture some of the joy and awe and worship and love and (yes) submission that grows from what the Bible says about holiness.

May God lead us to know him, love him, worship him, enjoy him, and serve him—and so prepare us for the holy courts of heaven.

Carolyn Nystrom

---

[1]John and Charles Wesley, *Selected Prayers, Hymns, Journal Notes, Sermons, Letters and Treatises* (New York: Paulist Press, 1981), pp. 301-4.

ONE

CALLED TO BE HOLY

Hebrews 12:14-29

Mike has a new job. Mike had always been a good worker. He got excellent reviews from his boss. But his job was a middle-management position that was eliminated by a company reorganization. They gave him severance pay, a good recommendation, and a pat on the back. It took Mike a year to find a job with a similar salary. In the meantime, Mike sent out résumés by day and stocked grocery shelves at night.

Mike's new job has him representing his company's products throughout the eastern half of the United States. He spends much of his week in airports and hotels.

Company clients expect a certain type of entertainment, and Mike's company expects him to please his clients. Most of these expectations do not conflict in any way with Mike's moral values. Mike sends flowers and fruit baskets at appropriate times, takes clients to dinner, provides theater tickets, and occasional limo service. And he is careful to send appreciative notes and letters.

But occasionally, Mike faces conflict between the demands of his job and his own desire to live by Christian principles. First, Mike wonders if it is "right" to spend so much time away from his family. Also, Mike is expected to put his company products in the best possible light. This sometimes goes beyond the limits of what Mike believes to be honest. Finally, a few clients expect entertainment that offends Mike's Christian sensitivities. Should he pay for a client to get drunk? Provide tickets to a play that he believes is obscene? Spend enough money for a week's supply of groceries on a single meal?

Mike wants to live a holy life. But he lives and works in an unholy world. What does his loving God expect from him?

Part One
1. What image does the word *holy* bring to your mind? (Think of both positive and negative images.)

Read Hebrews 12:14-29.
2. Notice the various descriptions of God in this passage. How does each of these descriptions begin to answer the universal question, "Who is God?"

3. What mixture of approachability and unapproachability do you see in these descriptions of God?

4. *The New Bible Dictionary* describes people who are holy as those who are "pure," "consecrated to God," those who have "moral excellence," or a "Christ-like character."[1] This passage opens with the command to "be holy." How might the character of God, as he is described here, inspire you to try to obey that command?

5. Look more carefully at verses 14-17. Why might the examples here of right and wrong ways to live motivate you to live in a holy way?

*6. Review Esau's story in Genesis 25:24-34 and 27:34-41. Who did Esau view too lightly? (himself? his brother? his father? God?) Explain.

*7. A Hebrew birthright came from God through the father who prayed a blessing on his oldest son. Why do you think the writer of Hebrews called Esau "godless"?

8. Study Hebrews 12:18-21. The *Jerusalem Bible* begins verse 18, "What you have come to is nothing known to the senses." As a contrast, how were all five senses active during the experience of the people at Mt. Sinai?

9. How does the description of Mt. Sinai help you to sense God's holiness?

*10. Hebrews 12:21 quotes Moses as saying, "I am trembling with fear." Review Exodus 19:10-23. Do you think that Moses' fear was appropriate? Explain.

11. What could you do to show more reverence for the holiness of God?

Part Two
*12. What attracts you to God?

Read Hebrews 12:14-29.
13. Verses 22-24 describe Mt. Zion as a contrast to Mt. Sinai. None of the phrases here can be perceived through our senses. What descriptive words and phrases give you clues about Mt. Zion?

14. What do you look forward to about your own presence in this "heavenly Jerusalem"?

15. What aspects of God's grace do you see in the description of Mt. Zion?

*16. Hebrews 12:24 contrasts Christ's blood with the blood of Abel. Review Genesis 4:8-12. What contrast do you see between what the blood of Abel said and what the blood of Jesus Christ says?

*17. Mt. Sinai pictures God's holiness while Mt. Zion emphasizes God's grace. Yet Hebrews 12:14-15 says that we must experience both. How does an understanding of God's holiness help you to experience his grace?

18. Hebrews 12:25-27 continues the comparison between God at Mt. Sinai and God at Mt. Zion. It speaks of both events as a warning. What warnings do you take from these verses?

19. Verse 27 further describes the judgment of God that was introduced in verse 23. Do you find God's promise to remove "what can be shaken" a worry or a reassurance? Why?

20. Hebrews 12:28-29 opens with the word *therefore,* a clue that the writer is about to make a concluding statement. As you study his conclusion, what seems to be the point of what the writer of Hebrews has said thus far in this section?

*21. Immediately after God gave Moses the Ten Commandments on Mt. Sinai, Moses explained to the people why God had revealed himself to them in such a fearsome way. Read Exodus 20:18-21. How might even this secondhand experience of God's holiness influence your own attempts at holy living?

22. Meditate on Hebrews 12:29: "Our God is a consuming fire." What unholy impurities do you hope that the fire of God will consume from your own life?

*optional question

---

[1]J. D. Douglas, *The New Bible Dictionary* (Wheaton, Ill.: Tyndale, 2d ed., 1982), p. 530.

TWO

HONESTY

Genesis 20; Psalm 15

C an I borrow the car tonight?"

"To go where?"

"To Kathy's."

"For?"

"Her mom wants me to move a load of compost into the flower beds like I did last year."

"And where else will you go?"

"Nowhere. Kathy and I will probably rent a movie."

"What movie?"

"How should I know? We haven't talked about it yet."

"Is it okay with her mom?"

"Yes, she called me today."

"And you aren't going anywhere except to Kathy's?"

"Right. Isn't that what I just said?"

A typical parent/teen conversation. The teen wants as much freedom as he can get—including planning his own itinerary and use of the family car. The parent wants to ensure safety—for both the car and the son, not to mention Kathy.

But past deceptions have undermined trust. The parent has become an inquisitor. The son has become an "artful dodger." And the son's real plans include a brief stop at Kathy's—and a lot of other "cruising." So his request includes a couple of small lies—and a lot of deception. His goal is to get what he wants—the family car. With any luck, he may even earn some bonus points with his parent for his alleged generosity in moving the compost.

But a lie contaminates everyone close to it. Trust falters. Relationships fray. Worst of all, it rots the character of the person who tells the lie.

Abraham, in 2000 B.C., encountered a situation where a lie seemed like the best choice. But God didn't agree.

1. What kinds of situations and/or relationships make truth-telling hard for you?

Read Genesis 20.
2. What is your initial reaction to each character in this story?

3. What does Abraham's lie (v. 2) reveal about his personal values?

4. Study God's words in verses 3 and 6-7. What do these statements reveal about God's values?

*5. Why do you think that Sarah agreed to this deception?

6. What potential harm might have come from Abraham's dishonesty?

7. How does God show that he cares for the various people touched by Abraham's lie (vv. 3-7)?

8. How does Abimelech show more concern for godly values than Abraham did?

*9. Why do you think that God talked to Abimelech, but not to Abraham?

10. What do you think of Abraham's reasons for lying to Abimelech (vv. 10-13)?

11. If Abraham's statement of verse 12 is true, would you say that Abraham lied to Abimelech? Explain.

*12. In what areas of your life do you need to be more honest?

Part Two
*13. What harm comes from lying? (Harm to the person receiving the lie? Harm to the person who lies?)

Read Genesis 20:1-18.
14. Look at God's instructions to Abimelech in verse 7. How did Abimelech go beyond even what God asked him to do (vv. 8-16)?

15. Read Genesis 18:10-19. How does this recent event in Abraham's past make his lie to Abimelech more serious?

16. Look more carefully at Genesis 18:18-19. In view of God's expectations for Abraham, how do you think Abraham ought to have handled the situation with Abimelech differently?

*17. Abimelech said to Sarah, "You are completely vindicated" (Gen 20:16). Who vindicated Sarah? How and why?

18. What did Abraham gain from his experience with Abimelech?

What did he lose?

***19.** What do you think Abraham, Abimelech and Sarah each learned from this experience?

Read Psalm 15.
***20.** What, according to this psalm, keeps a person from being shaken?

***21.** How might this psalm help you to make specific choices for honesty in your dealings with other people?

22. What forms of self-discipline would you recommend to someone who wanted to become more truthful?

23. What help in being honest do you need from your Christian friends?

from God?

*optional question

THREE

SELF-CONTROL

Judges 16; James 3:1-12

*I*n those days there was no king in Israel; every man did what was right in his own eyes."

This is the closing statement of one of the most tumultuous eras in the history of Israel. From approximately 1200 B.C. to about 1050 B.C., a series of judges ruled local clans of Hebrew people. But they never wholly possessed the land.

Though the Hittites had vanished by that time, the Hebrews warred with Canaanites, remnants of the local population. They mainly avoided the Phoenicians in their cities on the Mediterranean coast, but the Hebrews defeated the Moabites on the east bank of the Dead Sea. (They may have lost the entire tribe of Reuben in the process.) And the Hebrews had constant military and cultural skirmishes with the Philistines, who were local descendants of Egyptian loyalists and mercenary fighters of the previous century. Sometimes the Hebrews even fought each other.

The book of Judges creates a brief snapshot of events of this turbulent era. In it we see the Hebrew, Ehud, slaughter the overweight King Eglon of Moab by thrusting a sword so deep into his belly that the fat closed over the handle and Ehud could not withdraw his weapon.

We see Jael, a Hebrew woman, lure the Canaanite enemy Sisera into her tent, giving the thirsty fugitive goat's milk to drink and lulling him to sleep. Then, she put a tent peg through his temple, and pounded his head to the ground.

Into this chaotic national scene burst Samson. Samson was born to devout Hebrew parents who promised to give their child to God's service. But the young adult Samson fell in love with a Philistine woman, forced both families to accept marriage, then slaughtered thirty of his in-law's side of the bridal party because of a lost bet. Not surprisingly, his father-in-law cancelled the marriage. So Samson caught three hundred foxes, set them on fire, and turned them loose among Philistine ripened-grain fields.

In an era that specialized in lack of self-control, Samson must have seemed like a bawdy choir boy. But when everyone did only what was "right in his own eyes," the country suffered. So did the people in it.

Part One
1. What kinds of problems occur when someone lacks self-control?

Read Judges 16:1-22.
2. What examples of Samson's failure to exercise self-control can you see in this text?

*3. How do verses 1-3 help you to estimate Samson's strength?

4. What mental images does the account of Samson's various escapades create for you?

5. What do Delilah's attempts to discover the source of Samson's strength, and Samson's response to these attempts, suggest about the relationship between these two people?

*6. Why do you think Delilah treated Samson the way she did?

*7. What character qualities in Samson made it possible for Delilah to keep her part of the bargain?

8. How do you feel when you read the words of verses 20-21? Why?

*Read Judges 16:23-31.
*9. In what ways did the Philistines humiliate Samson?

*10. Was Samson's death a suicide?

*11. Study the words of Samson's prayer of verse 28. What does it suggest about Samson's moral and spiritual condition?

*12. Would you say that Samson put self-control to good or bad use in the ending of this story? Explain.

13. Think about a time that you failed to exercise self-control. How did this affect your relationships? (Consider what this says about how you regard yourself, others and God.)

Part Two
*14. What kinds of damage come from words that lack self-control?

15. When have you wished that you could "eat your words"?

Read James 3:1-12.
16. Verse 2 says, "If anyone is never at fault in what he says he is . . . able to keep his whole body in check." Why is the use of the tongue such a good test for self-control?

17. Notice the different objects this text uses to illustrate control. How do these further define the use of the tongue?

18. What inconsistencies do verses 7-12 point out?

19. How do the fig tree, grapevine, and salt spring illustrate the tongue?

20. Verse 8 speaks of the tongue as containing "deadly poison." When have you seen words become deadly poison?

21. Verse 9 says that blessing may come from the tongue. When have you been "blessed" by someone's tongue?

*22. Verse 1 begins, "Not many of you should presume to be teachers." How might this passage help a person, who does presume to teach, to become a better teacher?

23. In what areas of your life would you like to gain more self-control—so that you could more consistently bless both God and people?

*24. What are the pressure points that cause you to lose self-control?

25. How can your believing friends pray for you as you try to gain self-control during those pressured times?

*optional question

FOUR

SEXUAL PURITY

Genesis 2:18-25; Genesis 39; 1 Corinthians 6:12-20

*M*arried for two years, our daughter, Sheri, and son-in-law, Joel, were a cameo picture of young love. Bright, vivacious, playful, their days sparkled with laughter, dampened with only the barest sprinkle of weepy sighs. They loved and served their Lord with the same enthusiasm they lavished on each other. She finished college. He finished graduate school. First careers waited in the wings. In just over five months, they would be new parents. Their world fairly danced with anticipation.

That world ended on a bright sunny morning when a car accident took the lives of both Sheri and her baby. On Monday, Joel was an expectant father with a pretty, affectionate wife. On Tuesday, he was a twenty-five-year-old widower with restless hormones and grinding loneliness.

"Don't make any major decisions for a year," wise elders counseled. "Give yourself time to grieve."

Joel nodded agreement. But in private he wondered aloud, "How can I stay single for a whole year?"

"Sure, you will marry again," consoled a woman friend. "But wouldn't it be a great wedding gift to your new wife to be celibate until you marry her?"

But other women suggested easier routes. "If you *need* anything," said one, "I'm often home alone," as she swayed off into the evening.

Three years later, Joel remains single—and celibate. He has lived with other single guys. He works, continues to worship in church, and has started another graduate degree. Over time he has also cultivated friendships (romantic and otherwise) with young women.

"Sexual purity is not easy for a young widower," he says. "But it is not impossible. A harder problem is the loneliness. And I think that a 'quick fix' to sexual pressure would only make the loneliness worse. So, I'll keep on waiting."

Part One
1. What pressures make it hard for people to maintain sexual purity?

*Read Genesis 2:18-25.
*2. What mental images do you see as you read this account?

*3. What was Adam's problem?

*What all did God do to help Adam recognize that problem—and then solve it for him?

*4. This passage is often read at weddings. How might the principles expressed in the text contribute to a healthy marriage?

*5. How could this passage contribute to a healthy view of sexuality?

Joseph, eleventh of Jacob's twelve sons (and his father's favorite), was hated by his elder brothers. With the hope of getting rid of him, the brothers dumped him into a pit, then sold him to nomadic traders—who took him to Egypt and resold him to Potiphar, the captain of Pharaoh's guard troops. There Joseph had to make some decisions about how (and whether) to improve his position.

Read Genesis 39:1-23.
*6. What evidences could Joseph see that God was taking care of him?

7. What forms of sexual harassment did Joseph have to cope with from Potiphar's wife (vv. 7-19)?

8. What steps did Joseph take to resist that harassment?

9. In verse 9, Joseph explained to Potiphar's wife why he refused to sleep with her. What values undergird those reasons?

*10. How did Joseph's behavior reflect the values you saw in the creation events of Genesis 2?

11. Joseph did the "right" thing, yet he landed in jail. What does this suggest about the practical aspects of sexual purity?

12. If a person today decides to practice sexual purity, what can he or she expect to give up?

What can he or she expect to gain?

Part Two
*13. What do you like and not like about your body?

Read 1 Corinthians 6:12-20.

14. In what different ways throughout this text does Paul show that our bodies are important?

*15. Why does Paul compare sex to food (vv. 12-13)?

16. Verse 13 says, "The body is not meant for sexual immorality, but for the Lord." Why might using your body for sexual immorality limit your ability to serve God?

*17. Verse 14 speaks of resurrection, Christ's and ours. How might a belief in the resurrection of the body encourage you toward sexual purity?

18. In verse 16, Paul quotes the Genesis creation passage, "The two shall become one flesh." What new significance does Paul bring to this ancient text?

*19. Verse 18 says that sexual sins are sins against our own bodies. What personal harm can come from these sins?

20. What does a temple symbolize in your mind?

21. Think again about God's creation of the human body. Why do you think God chooses to inhabit the bodies of his believers rather than created objects such as rocks and trees and clouds?

22. Verse 19 says, "You are not your own." How is this statement in conflict with current secular ethics?

*23. What practical differences result from these two opposite views of the self?

24. Verse 18 begins, "Flee from sexual immorality." In what practical ways can a person who wants to keep sexually pure limit sexual temptations?

25. Look again at Paul's closing statement of this chapter. How can you better honor God with your body?

*optional question

FIVE

INTEGRITY

Job 1:1—2:10; Psalm 25

*I*n Philip Yancey's thoughtful book, *Disappointment with God*, the writer speaks of Richard—a new and enthusiastic convert to the Christian faith. Richard studied the Bible with diligence and prayed every day. He transferred from a university to a Christian college, graduated, and went on to a Christian graduate school. There he wrote a paper about the biblical book of Job, a paper so far better than normal student fare that his professor recommended publication. With help from Yancey, that paper became a book.

But something went wrong for Richard. The student who wrote about Job, began to live a little of Job's life. It began when he attended a healing service. He watched a man, a doctor with lung cancer, be carried to the stage on a stretcher. The man walked away, praising God and feeling great. A week later, Richard called the doctor to continue praising God with him. The man's subdued wife announced, "My husband died this week."

Then Richard's parents separated. Richard dropped out of school for a while to try to mend his family. He prayed constantly that God would bring his parents back together. His parents remained apart.

Next Richard lost an important job. Then his fiancée jilted him. And his health began to deteriorate.

One night, Richard stayed up all night to pray. For four hours he pleaded with God to reveal himself. Nothing. Finally, Richard got up from his knees, gathered up his Bible and his theology textbooks, and went out to a backyard brick barbecue. There, in the last hours of darkness, Richard burned his books—and his faith.

Why? As Yancey said, "The theology he had learned in school and had written about in his book no longer *worked for him*." He was disappointed with God.

But is faith in God good only as long as it "works"?

Eons ago, that question came up in the courts of heaven. And the question asker was Satan.

Part One

1. When have you felt disappointed with God?

Read Job 1:1—2:10.

2. What reasons did Job have to feel that God had let him down?

3. What information was hidden from Job?

*4. What can you know, from this passage, about Satan's purpose and character?

*5. What reasons did Job have to believe that God was pleased with him (1:1-5)?

6. What accusation did Satan make about Job's motives for righteous living (1:9-11)?

7. What are some of your own motives for serving God? (Be honest.)

8. In view of Satan's accusations about Job, how might we sin even though we *do* all of the right things?

*9. If God "owed" Job protection from Satan, what would that debt suggest about the relationship between Job and God?

10. Study Job's words and actions in 1:20-22 and 2:9-10. What do these reveal about Job's view of his relationship with God?

*11. What do you think of Job's wife?

12. In Job 2:3, God described Job to Satan by saying, "And he still maintains his integrity." In 2:9, Job's wife threw his integrity at him as an accusation. How did Job's motives for serving God reveal his integrity?

13. Job expressed integrity in a number of ways. Which of these would you like to see more in yourself?

Part Two
*14. When you are in a difficult situation, what kind of prayer are you likely to pray to God?

Read Psalm 25.
*15. Psalm 25 divides into four stanzas. Give a topic-title to each (vv. 1-3, 4-7, 8-15, 16-22).

16. What does it meant to "lift up" your soul to God?

17. Study stanza 2. What all does David ask God to do?

*18. In what ways do David's requests reflect his continuing worship?

*19. Three times David uses the term "remember." Why would David want God to use "selective memory"?

20. What would you want God to remember (and not remember) about you?

21. Study stanza 3. David began his prayer by saying that he trusted God. In what ways does stanza 3 show that God has integrity—and therefore ought to be trusted?

*22. In what ways does this stanza acknowledge David's dependence on God?

23. What do you count on God to do and to be?

24. Study stanza 4. What words and phrases here help you to understand David's current situation?

25. Compare David's position, described in stanza 4, with what he hopes from God in verses 12-13. In view of the differences, what does David's prayer say about his own integrity?

26. David closes his prayer by saying, "May integrity and uprightness protect me because my hope is in you." How might meditating on God's character, as David did, help you to strengthen your own integrity?

*optional question

SIX

FACING TEMPTATION

Leviticus 16:3-34; Romans 8:1-17

I haven't sinned for seventeen years," says one fervent Christian. "I sin every day," says another, equally fervent.

These two Christians may define "sin" differently, but each knows the insistent battle of temptation. One knows the constant guardedness it takes to resist a small lie, a cutting remark, an inclination to laziness. The other knows the equally constant wash of God's grace as confession assures forgiveness and a continued walk with Christ.

The first would feel at home with the theology of John Wesley, who said, "For as he loves God, so he *keeps his commandments:* Not only *some*, or *most* of but ALL, from the least to the greatest. He is not content to *keep the whole law, and offend in one point*, but has in all points a *conscience void of offense, toward God, and toward man*. Whatever God has forbidden he avoids, whatever God has enjoined he does. . . . It is his glory and joy to do so."[1]

The second would appreciate Charles Hodge's view:

The thing to be done is to turn from sin to holiness; to love God perfectly and our neighbour as ourselves; to perform every duty without defect or omission, and keep ourselves from all sin of thought, word, or deed, of heart or life. Can any man do this? Does any man need argument to convince him that he cannot do it? He knows two things as clearly and as certainly as he knows his own existence: first, that he is bound to be morally perfect, to keep all God's commands, to have all right feelings in constant exercise as the occasion calls for them and to avoid all sin in feeling as well as in act; and, secondly, that he can no more do this than he can raise the dead."[2]

But no matter which theologian matches a person's concept of the sin-battle, both people mentioned above love Jesus Christ and want to serve him. And each knows that temptation is Satan's constant attempt to come between us and our Lord.

Part One

1. What do you do when you feel guilty about something?

Read Leviticus 16:3-34.

2. As you visualize all that was to happen on the Day of Atonement, what pictures remind you that God is holy and that he expects holiness from his people?

*3. Divide the ritual for the Day of Atonement into sections. (Paragraphs are good indicators.) What was done at each stage?

4. What personal preparation was Aaron to make for his work of atonement (vv. 1-14)?

5. What did this preparation symbolize about Aaron and his role before God and his people?

6. Notice the five sacrificial animals. What was the purpose of each?

7. How is each goat a visual symbol of sin?

*8. Why do you think that God commanded both confession and sacrifice?

*9. What all did the worship leaders do to symbolize the close of the atonement ceremony (vv. 23-28)?

10. What practical good could come from this method of atoning for sin?

What limitations do you see to this kind of atonement?

11. Imagine yourself as a Hebrew of this era. How do you think you would feel on the days just before and just after the Day of Atonement?

Do you think you would participate in this yearly event? Explain.

Part Two
12. What circumstances make you vulnerable to temptation?

Read Romans 8:1-17.
13. Verse 1 says, "Therefore, there is now no condemnation." Why?

*14. In what ways was Christ like both of the goats from Leviticus 16—the sin-offering and the scapegoat?

15. Verses 1-4 speak of all three persons of the Trinity. What part does each member play in offering a solution to human sinfulness?

16. In verses 5-8, Paul describes two mindsets—those who set their minds on "what nature desires," and those who set their minds on "what the Spirit desires." What words and phrases describe the results of each mindset?

17. When have you seen these kinds of results?

18. Study verses 9-11. What reasons for hope do you find here?

19. Reread verses 12-17. What different kinds of death does this passage address?

20. What do you find inviting about the relationship with God described here?

*21. How might the relationship with God, as it is described here, help you to resist temptation?

22. Review all of Romans 8:1-17 noting each mention of God's Holy Spirit. What forms of help does God offer through his Spirit?

23. Think again about situations that make you vulnerable to temptation. In view of the promised work of the Holy Spirit in your life, how might you best prepare to meet and resist those temptations?

* optional question

[1]Wesley, p. 305.   [2]Charles Hodge, *Romans,* vol. 2 (Edinburgh: The Banner of Truth Trust), p. 271.

Leader's Notes

Leading a Bible discussion can be an enjoyable and rewarding experience. But it can also be intimidating—especially if you've never done it before. If this is how you feel, you're in good company. When God asked Moses to lead the Israelites out of Egypt, he replied, "O Lord, please send someone else to do it!" (Ex 4:13). But God's response to all of his servants—including you—is essentially the same: "My grace is sufficient for you" (2 Cor 12:9).

There is another reason you should feel encouraged. Leading a Bible discussion is not difficult if you follow certain guidelines. You don't need to be an expert on the Bible or a trained teacher. The suggestions listed below should enable you to effectively and enjoyably fulfill your role as leader. And remember the discussion leader usually learns the most—so lead and grow!

Preparing for the Study

Group leaders can prepare to lead a group by following much the same pattern outlined for individual study at the beginning of this guide. Try to begin preparation far enough in advance for the Spirit of God to begin to use the passage in your own life. Then you will have some idea about what group members will experience as they attempt to live out the passage. Advance preparation will also give your mind time to thoughtfully consider the concepts—probably in odd moments when you least expect it.

Study the flow of the questions. Consider the time available. Plan for an appropriate break (if you are using two sessions) and which optional questions you will use. Note this in your study guide so that you will not feel lost in the middle of the discussion. But be ready to make changes "en route" if the pattern of discussion demands it. Pencil near the questions any information from the leader's section that you don't want to forget. This will eliminate clumsy page turns in the middle of the discussion.

And pray. Pray for each person in the group—by name. Ask that God will prepare that person, just as he is preparing you, to confront the truths of this passage of his Word.

During the Study

1. One of the major jobs of the discussion leader is to pace the study. Don't make your job more difficult by beginning late. So keep an eye on the clock. When the agreed time to begin arrives, launch the study.

2. Take appropriate note of the introductory essay, then ask the approach question. Encourage each of the group members to respond to the question. When everyone is involved in discussing the general topic of the day, you are ready to explore the Scripture.

3. Read the passage aloud, or ask others to read aloud—by paragraphs, not verses. Verse-by-verse reading breaks the flow of thought and reduces understanding. And silent reading often makes concentration difficult, especially for people who are distracted by small noises or who are uncomfortable with group silence. So read aloud—by paragraphs.

4. Keep in mind that the leader's job is to help a group to discover together the content, meaning and implications of a passage of Scripture. People should focus on each other and on the Bible—not necessarily on you. Your job is to moderate a discussion, to keep conversation from lagging, to draw in quiet members, and to pace the study. So encourage multiple responses to questions, and encourage people to interact with each other's observations. Volunteer your own answers only in similar proportion to others in the group.

5. Pacing is a major difficulty for inexperienced leaders. Most group participants have set obligations after a scheduled Bible study. You will earn their thanks if you close the study at a predictable time. But to do so you don't want to race ahead and miss details in the early questions; nor do you want to play catch-up at the end: skipping sections people most want to talk about. Try writing in your study guide the time that you hope to finish questions at various points in the study. This will help you keep a steady pace. Note also any optional questions that you can add or subtract, depending on the pace of the study. But be alert to particular needs and interests in the group. Sometimes you should abandon even the best-laid plans in order to tend to these.

6. If possible, spend time talking about personal needs and praying together. Many groups begin or end by speaking of various worries, concerns, reasons for thanksgiving—or just their plans for the week. Groups who pray together often see God at work in ways far beyond their expectations. It's an excellent way to grow in faith.

7. If you have time, do some further reading on small groups and the dynamics of such groups. For a short, but helpful, overview read *Leading Bible Discussions* by James Nyquist and Jack Kuhatschek (InterVarsity Press). Or for a more in-depth discussion read *Small Group Leaders' Handbook* or *Good Things Come in Small Groups*, both of which are edited by Ron Nicholas (InterVarsity Press). For an excellent study of how small groups can contribute to spiritual growth read *Pilgrims in Progress* by Jim and Carol Plueddemann (Harold Shaw).

The following notes refer to specific studies in the guide:

Study 1. Called to Be Holy. Hebrews 12:14-29.
Purpose: To desire holy living in ourselves because of God's revelation of his own character.

Question 1. Use this question to involve as many people as possible in the conversation. Be sure to treat both positive and negative images of holiness. A few anecdotes to illustrate these images will make your discussion more lively.

Question 2. Study the descriptions of God in verses 14, 15, 22, 23, 24, 28 and 29. Discuss what each description reveals about God's nature. Discussion, at this point, should be brief. You will answer this question in more depth later in the study as you concentrate on each paragraph.

Question 3. Encourage people to cite phrases and verse numbers that suggest either God's approachability or his unapproachability. The passage contains numerous examples of each.

Question 5. Use this question to study the first paragraph of the text in greater detail, then to respond to it in a personal way.

Question 6. It is possible that Esau viewed everyone mentioned in this question too lightly. Encourage group members to show how Esau underestimated each—and how he undervalued the rights that belonged to him because he was "firstborn." An allusion to the position that Esau gave up comes again in Hebrews 12:23 when believers in Jesus who arrive at the heavenly Jerusalem are called the "church of the firstborn."

Question 7. Verse 16 suggests that by giving up his birthright, Esau showed that he was godless. As we have seen, he showed disrespect for the privilege God had granted him.

Bible scholars have written much more about why Esau was termed "godless" and just what that means. Many other questions may be raised. What exactly did Esau give up? Why was he crying? Repentance? Regret? Dismay at a loss that he finally understood? Why was he unable to regain his birthright? And most important, what does the Esau story teach about Christians who have access to God's family—and later reject that relationship?

This text is insufficient to answer all of those questions—even though it raises them. So don't expect your group to resolve them with any satisfaction. The best tack is to discuss the question a bit, accept it as another in a series of biblical mysteries, and proceed with the study.

Question 8. Study the text to discover what the Hebrews at Mt. Sinai would have seen, heard, felt, tasted, touched.

Question 9. Let people in the group explore their personal reactions to this sensory information about God.

Question 11. Encourage each person to express some personal response to God's holiness. They may discuss ways of showing more reverence in group worship, private prayer or obedient living. They may decide to stop trying to manipulate God—as if by some magic formula of prayer or deeds, they could get God to give them what they want. The holy God of Mt. Sinai is not a tool to be used at our whim and convenience. Help participants to be as personal and specific in their resolutions as is possible for the confidence level of your group.

If you are dividing your study into two sessions, end session one at this point.

Question 12. If you are using this study for two sessions, begin session two with this question. Then re-read aloud Hebrews 12:14-29.

Try to involve each person with a response to this question. If you need to break the question down into smaller portions, ask, "What in yourself attracts you to God?" and "What in God attracts you to him?"

Question 13. Use this question to study the details of verses 22-24. Discuss what some of these intangible descriptions of the Mount Zion might mean. Descriptive terms include "heavenly Jerusalem," "city of the living God," "joyful assembly," "church of the firstborn," "judge of all men," "spirits of righteous men," "Jesus the mediator," and "new covenant." Each of these terms is rich with meaning—but nothing that we can touch, taste, see, hear or smell.

Question 15. You will have begun to work on this question as you discussed question 13. Now study it in more detail. If you need a quick definition of grace, try "undeserved favour by a superior to an inferior" (Sinclair Ferguson and D. F. Wright, eds., *The New Dictionary of Theology* [Downers Grove, Ill.: InterVarsity Press, 1988], p. 280).

Question 18. Help your group members to study the details of verses 25-27, then draw conclusions about what personal warning they might take from this text.

Question 19. Expect both kinds of answers here. If God's judgment removes what can be shaken, only what is solid remains. Yet many of us feel shaky much of the time—even without this kind of upheaval. And we depend, for our security, on things that we know can be shaken (job, money, family, church, friends, ourselves). So we may find this kind of promised judgment unsettling at best. Yet there is also something reassuring about the idea that it is God himself who will do the shaking, and that he will discover what is solid. And that he, himself, will remain. God is a part of what is unshakable. And ultimately, the believer's trust is in him.

Question 20. This passage from Hebrews opens with a call to holy living. Though the word *holy* is not mentioned at the end, it closes in much the same way. If we are to worship God with "reverence and awe" (because he is holy), part of our worship will include holy living. That which is not holy will be "shaken" and purged by the "consuming fire."

Question 21. God's character, revealed in his holiness at Mt. Sinai and also his grace in the promised Mt. Zion, ought to inspire us to holy obedience. Help your group to think of practical, appropriate responses to this revelation of God's character.

Question 22. Be personal here. Cite examples from your own life that you want to subject to God's cleansing. Encourage your group to do the same.

Note: The quotation in Hebrews 12:29 ("Our God is a consuming fire") came as a reaction to the experience on Mt. Sinai. See Exodus 24:17.

Study 2. Honesty. Genesis 20; Psalm 15.

Purpose: To acknowledge the temptation to lie, and to seek help in becoming more honest in our actions and words.

Question 1. Even though this involves some measure of confession, it is good at this point to acknowledge that we are tempted. Almost everyone has told a lie at one time or another, and most of us know what settings most tempt us in that direction.

The responses can be pretty general, but try to get a response from each person. Expect such answers as:

☐ When I want to tell a story and make it more interesting than it is.

☐ When I want someone to think better of me than I think of myself.

☐ When I want to brag about my kids, I am tempted to stretch the truth a bit.

☐ When I want to stay out of trouble.

☐ When my husband/wife asks me if I've done something that I should have, but didn't.

☐ When I want to protect someone else from knowing something that would make them feel bad.

☐ When someone asks me, "How are you." And I say, "Fine."

Make mental or jotted notes about people's areas of temptation. Help them refer to them again as a part of the response to question 12.

If this question seems too personal to open a discussion with your group, try, "When have you seen a relationship damaged by deceit?"

Question 2. Gain surface responses here to Abraham, Sarah and Abimelech. Later questions will help you discuss these characters in more detail.

Question 3. Your group should look at Abraham's relative concern for Sarah, Abimelech, Abimelech's people, and himself. His action appears to have put more value on himself than on anyone else, a frequent source of lying. A follow-up question of supposition might be, "Did Abraham love his wife?"

Question 6. Discuss a variety of potential problems for each of the characters in the story.

Question 8. Study Abimelech's words and actions. Compare these with what you know of godly principles.

Question 10. Abraham explains himself in verses 11 and 12. Let people in your group devise their own evaluations of his motives.

Note: Abimelech's actions reveal that he seems to have much more fear of God than Abraham realized.

Question 11. Was Sarah really Abraham's half-sister? Information about Abraham's family appears in Genesis 11:27-32. But Sarah is mentioned only as his wife. Scripture does not elsewhere define her parentage. Even so, Abraham illustrates a universal problem for those who lie. Because of one lie, his word on similar subjects face disbelief. We feel, justifiably, that we must prove his words from some outside source. Four thousand years later, readers cannot *know* that Sarah was Abraham's half-sister—just because he said it.

For a follow-up question, ask, "What is the difference between a lie and a deception? Are both wrong? Explain."

Question 12. Refer back to the situations described in question 1. Help people in your group be specific about the situations in which they hope to become more honest.

If you are dividing this study into two portions, close section one after this question.

Question 13. If you are beginning a new study at this point, discuss this question, then re-read Genesis 20.

Question 14. Study Abimelech's conversation with God (vv. 4-5), his conversation with his officials and then with Abraham (vv. 8-10), and his subsequent actions (vv. 14-16). Discuss how these actions prevented some of the harm of Abraham's lie.

Question 17. Abimelech vindicated Sarah. So did God. But Abraham had little to do with it. Let your group speculate as to why Abimelech and God acted toward Sarah in the way that they did.

Question 18. Abraham gained all of the goods and opportunities described in verses 14-15. But he lost the trust of Abimelech and his people. He missed the opportunity to share his faith in the true God with a person who was not of his own ethnic origin. His relationship with Sarah was damaged. God allowed him to pray for Abimelech and his people, but even though God had called Abraham to be the founder of his divinely chosen people, Abraham was now in no position to be a godly mentor to Abimelech.

You may wonder why God allowed Abraham to profit from his lie. Meredith G. Kline writing in *New Bible Commentary* says, "By his lavish gifts Abimelech would have Sarah forget her experience in his court. . . . In spite of indignity suffered, Sarah's honour was by the royal gift restored in the eyes of others" (p. 98).

And Gleason L. Archer, writing in *Encyclopedia of Bible Difficulties*, says:
Abraham showed a lack of confidence in God's power to preserve him from mortal danger and failed to uphold God's honor before the eyes of the unbelieving world. Even though he was given a thousand shekels by way of atonement for Abimelech's having taken Sarah into his palace, Abraham had to leave under a cloud of dishonor. . . . This account no more exonerates Abraham from his sin than did the similar adventure in Egypt. He came away from both failures with dishonor and shame, and his influence on the Philistines was as nullified as it had been in the case of the Egyptians." (p. 90)

Question 20. Survey the information in the psalm. People who were present for Study 1 will notice a correlation between the stability promised in this psalm and God's shaking judgment of Hebrews 12:28.

Question 21. Pace your study so that you leave adequate time for these final questions. Answers to this question may help people who have not voiced particular temptations to lie or deceive.

Question 23. This is a more personal question, and it broadens the issue to all forms of being honest. Responses may lead people to become accountable to each other in specific tempting situations. Close with prayers that worship God for his holiness and with prayers that support each person's commitments to overcoming dishonesty.

Study 3. Self-Control. Judges 16; James 3:1-12.

Purpose: To learn from biblical examples and teachings to exercise better self-control.

Question 1. Answers should include problems for people who do not exercise appropriate self-control, as well as problems occurring for the people around them. If you must subdivide the question in order to gain adequate responses ask, "When a person lacks self-control, what problems does he or she cause for other people?" "What problems does this person cause for himself or herself?"

Question 2. Use this question to provide a brief survey of the passage. You will treat it in detail later in the study.

Question 3. By consulting a map, your group will discover that the distance from Gaza to Hebron is about 38 miles. The text also mentions the *top* of the hill. We can only guess at the weight of the gates. But the method of removal, suggested in the text, involves more strength than tools.

Question 4. Discuss mental pictures of the four escapes (vv. 3, 9, 12, and 14).

Question 6. Delilah was offered a huge amount of money. According to *The NIV Study Bible* it would have been equivalent to the price of 275 slaves (p. 353). Sex, power, national loyalty, and revenge all might have also figured into Delilah's motives. Let group members defend their favorite possibilities.

Question 7. By now your group will feel like it knows Samson fairly well. Let people discuss how his own character and behavior flaws contributed to his downfall.

Question 8. Discussion of this question calls for an emotional rather than a rational response. Some may wonder, however, why Samson did not know that the Lord had left him (v. 20). Keil and Delitzsch comment as follows:

". . . but he knew not that Jehovah had departed from him." These last words are
very important to observe in order to form a correct idea of the affair.
Samson had said to Delilah, "If my hair were cut off, *my strength* would
depart from me" (ver. 17). The historian observes, on the other hand,
that *"Jehovah* had departed from him." The superhuman strength of
Samson did not reside in his hair as hair, but in the fact that Jehovah
was with or near him. But Jehovah was with him so long as he main-
tained his condition as a Nazirite. As soon as he broke away from this
by sacrificing the hair which he wore in honour of the LORD, Jehovah
departed from him, and with Jehovah went his strength." (vol 2, p. 423)
You may also wonder what it meant to be a Nazirite. *The Zondervan Pictorial
Encyclopedia of the Bible* explains that a Nazirite was a member of a Hebrew
religious class especially dedicated to God. God gave instructions for this
order in Numbers 6:1-12, just before the Hebrews left Mt. Sinai.

Nazirites took voluntary vows, either in person or on the strength of
their parent's vows. They were not to touch any dead body. They were not
to use any grape products. (Grapes symbolized all of the temptations of a
settled life in Canaan.) And they were not to shave or cut their hair.

Some people took these vows for a limited period of time. The apostle
Paul did so in Acts 18:18. Others like Samuel, John the Baptist, and Samson
took vows that extended for a lifetime. Nazirites were to make themselves
always available for use by God. And he or she was to lead the people of
Israel in devotion to God (vol 4, pp. 392-93).

Question 10. This question will be likely to raise some ethical questions,
particularly surrounding the definition of suicide, or whether suicide is ever
morally right. It will not resolve all of these issues, but will raise questions
worthy of discussion. Question 12 will further enlarge this discussion.

Question 11. Study Samson's words in verse 28.

Question 13. Divide this question into two parts. Let several people respond
to the initial question. Then discuss the comments in the parentheses. Refusal to exercise self-control is at heart a selfish act. It sees personal expression as of greater worth than the damage that expression may inflict on
someone else. Therefore, lack of self-control says, "I am more important
than you are." Refusal to exercise self-control also underestimates God. It
says, "God is kind, he understands, he will forgive me." But it does not
properly apprehend God's holiness—or his judgment. And refusal to exercise self-control is self-indulgent. It is a lazy approach to life that says, "I am
what I am. Why change?" If you are dividing this study into two sessions,
end session one at this point and begin your new study with question 14.

Question 17. James uses a horse's bit, a ship's rudder, and a fire's spark as symbols of the tongue. Each controls a body much larger than itself. And the effects of a bit, a rudder, and a spark go far beyond their immediate locations. Everyone has, on occasion, felt astonished at the long-range effect of certain words—for both good and evil.

If you want a follow-up question, ask "Why do you think James uses these in connection with a lecture on the use of the tongue?"

Questions 18-19. Use these questions to examine the content and meaning of verses 7-12.

Question 22. Use the entire passage to respond to this question.

Question 25. Pray for each other for the specific situations mentioned. Let your prayers be brief, but highly personal.

Study 4. Sexual Purity. Genesis 2:18-25; Genesis 39; 1 Corinthians 6:12-20.
Purpose: To cultivate sexual purity because God created our bodies as a gift to our marriage partner and as his own temple.

Question 1. Encourage a variety of answers. The media is an easy target: TV ads, movies, pop music, TV shows, billboards, all shout sex at every turn. But encourage your group to discuss more subtle pressures. For example, there is the "couples only" pressure of many social groups—including churches—the peer pressure for early sexual experimentation among teens, the moral view that sexual behavior is a personal decision not to be regulated by rules or authority, the internal pressure felt by those who feel attraction to those of the same sex, and alternately, the pressure to *prove* "normal" sexual interest by performing early and often with the opposite sex, the general disintegration of marriage and family bonds, and the innate desire for intimacy in a world increasingly cluttered with rapid pace and shallow relationships.

Question 2. Survey the passage, at a visual level, with the question.

Question 3. Verse 18 mentions Adam's loneliness and also his need for help. Use the rest of the passage to answer the second half of the question. (Be sure that you treat both needs.)

Question 4. Several general principles of marriage emerge from this passage: Marriage can and should relieve loneliness; it should provide mutual help; it can unite people in such a way that they become part of each other—as though they were created from each other—a completion of what is not quite finished alone; marriage should create a joyful, unashamed, enjoyment of each other's bodies (they were both naked and felt no shame); marriage bonds take priority over all other relational ties, even the next closest bonds, those of parents.

Question 5. A further discussion of verses 23-25 will help at this point.

Question 6. Look at Genesis 39:2-6 and 21-23. Some may note that even though Joseph enjoyed many advantages that signified God's blessing, he was in fact a slave and a prisoner. Clearly, God's presence and blessing does not guarantee the easiest or most prestigious position. We see instead that Joseph worked and served well in the position to which he was assigned. And that God was with him—even in jail.

Question 8. Note Joseph's actions in verses 7-9.

Question 9. Study Joseph's values as they relate to his work, his employer (slave owner), and his God.

Question 10. Some of the values discussed in response to question 4 will come to play as you discuss this question. Joseph did not directly refer to the creation account. But he seemed to desire for Potiphar and his wife some of the same things that God desired for Adam and Eve. Perhaps Joseph also wanted these for himself—at some later and appropriate time.

Questions 11-12. Obeying God in sexual areas does not guarantee an easy life. God's rewards are not that direct. But your group should be able to discuss some of the positive and negative outgrowths of obedience in this area.

Don't hesitate to discuss what a person must give up to obey God in this area. We are more likely to pay the cost if we have first calculated what that cost is.

If you are dividing this study over two sessions, end session one at this point.

Question 13. Begin session two with this question. Brief jovial answers are appropriate. But try to maintain some level of honesty. If we are to accept the honor God gives our bodies as a temple of his Holy Spirit, we must see first how we treat (and mistreat) those bodies. Much of that treatment relates to what we like and don't like about our bodies in the first place.

If you need a less personal question to begin the study, ask, "What are some ways that you take care of your body?" Or, "What is one thing you have done this week to take care of your body?"

Question 14. Survey the passage with this question. Answers appear in nearly every verse.

Question 15. Both food and sex fulfill physical need. Both food and sex demand a measure of self-control—or they will control us. *NIV Study Bible* says:

> Food for the stomach and the stomach for food. Paul quotes some Corinthians again who were claiming that as the physical acts of eating and

digesting food have no bearing on one's inner spiritual life, so the physical act of promiscuous sexual activity does not affect one's spiritual life. The body is not meant for sexual immorality, but for the Lord. Paul here declares the dignity of the human body: It is intended for the Lord. Although granting that food and the stomach are transitory, Paul denies that what one does with his body is unimportant. This is particularly true of the use of sex, which the Lord has ordained in wedlock for the good of mankind (cf. Heb 13:4). (p. 1741)

Question 18. Use this question to study the content and meaning of verses 16-18.

Question 22. Current secular ethics teach that we belong to ourselves alone. We must take charge of our own lives. We must not allow others to manipulate us. We must first look at "What's in it for me?" If we don't take care of ourselves, no one else will.

Christian ethics, as expressed in this chapter and elsewhere, say that this is not true at all. We are not our own. We belong body and soul to Jesus Christ (vv. 19-20). Our bodies, and their sexual gifts, belong to our spouses, as Paul explains further into his argument (1 Cor 7:4-5). We are to love and care for each other, sharing our needs and our talents (1 Cor 12). We are to love our neighbor as much as we love ourselves (Mt 19:19).

Use this question to clarify these opposite sets of values.

Question 23. Discuss the practical differences in behavior that ought to grow out of the opposite values expressed in the previous question.

Question 24-25. Reserve enough time for each person to discuss practical ways to live out the teachings of these passages. Be as personal and specific as possible.

Study 5. Integrity. Job 1:1—2:10; Psalm 25.

Purpose: To use Job's integrity, and God's, as an example for our own.

Question 1. Try to involve each group member in a response to this question.

Question 2. Outrage is a frequent response to Job's suffering. Let your group express this. Then help them point out details of Job's losses that lead to that emotion. Look particularly at 1:13-19 and 2:7-9.

Question 3. Study the information in 1:6-12 and 2:1-6.

Question 4. Use the information discovered in the previous question to make deductions about Satan's character and purpose. *NIV Study Bible* comments as follows:

The relationship between God and man is not exclusive and closed. A third party intrudes, the great adversary (see chs 1-2). Incapable of contending with God hand to hand, power pitted against power, he is bent on frustrating God's enterprise embodied in the creation and centered on the God-man relationship. As tempter he seeks to alienate man from God (see Ge 3; Mt 4:1); as accuser (one of the names by which he is called, *satan*, means 'accuser') he seeks to alienate God from man (see Zec 3:1; Rev 12:9-10). His all-consuming purpose is to drive an irremovable wedge between God and man, to effect an alienation that cannot be reconciled. (p. 732)

Question 5. Note that people in ancient times often believed that material success proved that God was pleased with them. In addition, notice all that Job did that showed worship and obedience to God.

Question 6. Study the implied accusation of 1:9-11. It strikes, not at Job's actions, but at his motives for doing good.

Question 7. Pause for a response from each person here. Most of us serve God out of mixed motives. It is appropriate to mention, at this point, some motives that are less than noble. Do we serve God because it is expected in our church and family? Because we are worried about his judgment? Because we expect a reward in heaven? Because we want his favor here? At core, do we serve God out of a concern for "what's in it for me?"

Question 8. If you have adequately discussed the previous two questions, your group will now see that it is possible to do all the right things for all the wrong reasons. This is precisely the accusation Satan made against Job. Satan suggested that Job's acts of righteousness had nothing to do with worship of God. His righteous acts were simply a con game. He played by the rules in order to get what he wanted from his Superior Being.

The NIV Study Bible comments:

When God calls up the name of Job before the accuser and testifies to the righteousness of this one on the earth—this man in whom God delights—Satan attempts with one crafty thrust both to assail God's beloved and to show up God as a fool. True to one of his modes of operation, he accuses Job before God. He charges that Job's godliness is evil. The very godliness in which God takes delight is void of all integrity; it is the worst of all sins. Job's godliness is self-serving; he is righteous only because it pays. If God will only let Satan tempt Job by breaking the link between righteousness and blessing, he will expose the righteous man for the sinner he is.

It is the adversary's ultimate challenge. For if the godliness of the righteous man in whom God delights can be shown to be the worst of all sins, then a chasm of alienation stands between them that cannot be bridged. Then even redemption is unthinkable, for the godliest of men will be shown to be the most ungodly. God's whole enterprise in creation and redemption will be shown to be radically flawed, and God can only sweep it all away with awful judgment.

The accusation, once raised, cannot be removed, not even by destroying the accuser. So God lets the adversary have his way with Job (within specified limits) so that God and the righteous Job may be vindicated and the great accuser silenced. Thus comes the anguish of Job, robbed of every sign of God's favor so that God becomes for him the great enigma. (p. 732)

Question 9. God does not *owe* us anything. To suggest that this is possible, puts humans in control of God, which is unthinkable.

Question 12. Study Job's statements about God to help determine his motives—and the integrity behind those motives. Integrity involves not so much *what* we do but *why.* In this, at least, both God and Satan agreed.

Integrity is "uprightness, soundness of character, moral wholeness" *(New Concise Webster's Dictionary,* New York: Modern Publishing Co., 1987).

Question 13. If you are dividing this study over two sessions, end session one at this point.

Question 14. Begin session two with this question.

Question 16. Don't look for a single "correct" answer. Capture some of the ideals of worship as individuals express how they lift up their souls to God.

If you need a follow-up question, ask, "What relationship do you find between your *trust* in God and *hope?*"

Question 17. Study the verbs in verses 4-7.

Question 18. Here instead of asking God for help, David states his own intentions. Worship here is expressed in commitment and submission, in a desire to learn from God and to be directed by God.

Question 20. Conduct a personal, thoughtful discussion of this question. Then, if time permits a follow-up question, ask, "What are you saying about God (and yourself) when you ask that he not remember certain things?"

Question 21. Almost every phrase in verses 8-15 will contribute an answer to this question.

Question 22. Move the focus from God to David with this question.

Question 24. Study verses 16-22. Your group should point out such words as, "lonely," "afflicted," "troubles," "anguish," "affliction," "distress" and "enemies." You should also note David's need for "rescue" and "refuge."

Question 25. We do not know the details of David's circumstances, but his descriptive words suggest a Job-like condition. Yet, verses 12-13 reflect an entirely different expectation. Even though these expectations are not yet met (and may not ever come to pass) David continues to worship God and commit himself to God. Though he speaks of God's integrity, his prayer of worship and commitment also reflects his own.

Question 26. If you need a more pointed follow-up question, ask, "What specific aspects of God's character would you like to imitate in order to have more integrity in yourself?"

Of verse 21, *NIV Study Bible* says, "integrity and uprightness. Personified virtues. . . Pardon is not enough; David prays that God will enable him to live a life of unmarred moral rectitude—even as God is 'good and upright' (v. 8)."

Study 6. Facing Temptation. Leviticus 16:3-34; Romans 8:1-17.

Purpose: To recognize that sin is an affront to God's holiness, and, therefore, to allow God's Holy Spirit to help us resist temptation.

Question 1. Involve each person. Discuss feelings as well as actions. These situations may involve simple mistakes as well as outright sin.

Question 2. Use this question to create a quick visual survey of the passage. Discuss how these visual images helped the people to sense God's holiness—and his right to make demands on them. Save more detailed analysis of the passage for later questions.

Question 3. Use these or similar paragraph divisions: vv. 3-5, 6-10, 11-14, 15-17, 18-19, 20-22, 23-24a, 24b-25, and 26-28. Let your group give a general description of the activity in each.

Question 6. Find information about each sacrificial animal as follows: bull—vv. 11-14, first goat—vv. 15-19, second goat—vv. 22-24, two rams—vv. 3 and 24.

Question 7. Study each goat, how it was selected, what was done to it and why. Discuss what each action symbolized about sin—and its cleansing.

Question 10. Discuss these questions as thoroughly as time permits. They will help prepare for your discussion of Romans 8.

Question 11. If you are dividing your study into two sessions, consider adding the following as a closing question to the first session: "How does the ceremony for the Day of Atonement help you to see sin as a serious affront to God?"

Question 12. Begin the second session with this question. Jot brief notes of answers here. (Try to get something from each person.) You will use them again in the closing question.

Question 13. Draw a survey of answers from the text.

Question 14. *The NIV Study Bible* comments as follows: "two male goats for a sin offering. One was the usual sin offering . . . and the other a scapegoat. No single offering could fully typify the atonement of Christ. The one goat was killed, its blood sprinkled in the Most Holy Place and its body burned outside the camp (vv. 15, 27), symbolizing the payment of the price of Christ's atonement. The other goat, sent away alive and bearing the sins of the nation (v. 21), symbolized the removal of sin and its guilt" (p. 167).

Question 20. Linger long enough here for several people to speak of the hope they feel because of Christ's work. Day-to-day hope in spite of the pressures of life, hope in our battle against temptation, and hope for eternity all grow from this passage.

Question 22. The work of the Holy Spirit appears throughout Romans 8. Here are sample answers to this question:

v. 2. The Holy Spirit can set me free from the law of sin.

v. 4. The Holy Spirit can show me how to live in a way that pleases God.

v. 5. The Spirit has certain desires for me—and I can set my mind on those standards.

v. 9. I can allow God's Spirit to control me.

v. 9. The Spirit lives in me.

v. 11. The Spirit raised Jesus from the dead and can also raise my body from death.

v. 13. The Spirit can help me kill sin in my life.

v. 14. The Spirit can lead me.

v. 16. The Spirit assures me that I belong to God.

Question 23. Draw out thoughtful practical answers as the group members reflect again on areas where they are particularly vulnerable to temptation. Pray for each other. Ask God for an increased awareness of the Holy Spirit as he assists you in your struggle against sin.

Carolyn Nystrom lives in St. Charles, Illinois, with her husband, Roger, and an assortment of cats and kids and quilts. She has written over 55 Bible study guides and books for adults and children.

For Further Reading

Aharoni, Yohanan, and Michael Avi-Yonah. *The Macmillan Bible Atlas.* New York: Macmillan, 1977.

Alexander, Donald L., ed. *Christian Spirituality: Five Views of Sanctification.* Downers Grove: InterVarsity Press, 1988.

St. Augustine. *City of God.* 7 vols. Loeb Classical Library. Harvard: Harvard University Press.

Bellah, Robert N., et al. *Habits of the Heart.* Berkeley, Calif.: University of California Press, 1985.

Bonhoeffer, Dietrich. *The Cost of Commitment.* New York: Macmillan, 1963.

Bonhoeffer, Dietrich. *Life Together.* San Francisco: Harper and Row, 1976.

Bright, John. *A History of Israel,* 3d ed. Philadelphia: Westminster Press, 1981.

Bunyan, John. *Pilgrim's Progress.* Moody Classics. Chicago, Ill.: Moody Press, 1984.

Buttrick, George Arthur, gen. ed. *The Interpreter's Bible in Twelve Volumes.* New York and Nashville: Abingdon Press, 1954.

Comenius, J. A. *The Labyrinth of the World and the Paradise of the Heart.* Ann Arbor: University of Michigan, 1972.

Douglas, J. D. *The New Bible Dictionary.* Grand Rapids, Mich.: Eerdmans, 1962.

Ferguson, Sinclair B., and David F. Wright, eds. *New Dictionary of Theology.* Downers Grove: InterVarsity Press, 1988.

Friesen, Gary, and Robin Maxson. *Decison Making and the Will of God.* Portland, Ore.: Multnomah, 1985.

Gasque, W. Ward, ed. New International Greek Commentary. Grand Rapids, Mich.: Eerdmans, 1978-.

Godet, Frederick Louis. *Commentary on Romans.* Grand Rapids, Mich.: Kregel, 1977.

Guthrie, D., J. A. Motyer, A. M. Stibbs, D. J. Wiseman. *The New Bible Commentary, Revised.* Grand Rapids, Mich.: Eerdmans, 1970.

Havel, Vaclav. *The Power of the Powerless*. M. E. Sharpe, 1990.

Hodge, Charles. *Romans*. Edinburgh: The Banner of Truth Trust, 1972.

Hodge, Charles. *Systematic Theology*. Grand Rapids, Mich.: Eerdmans, 1981.

Hubbard, Robert L., Jr. *The Book of Ruth*. The New International Commentary on the Old Testament. Grand Rapids, Mich.: Eerdmans, 1988.

Kuhatschek, Jack. *Taking the Guesswork out of Applying the Bible*. Downers Grove, Ill.: InterVarsity Press, 1990.

Keil, C. F., and F. Delitzsch. *Commentary on the Old Testament in Ten Volumes*. Grand Rapids, Mich.: Eerdmans, 1980.

Kierkegaard, Søren. *Fear and Trembling*. Books on Demand UMI.

Lewis, C. S. *The Screwtape Letters*. Rev. ed. New York: Macmillan, 1982.

Lewis, C. S. *Surprised by Joy*. New York: Harcourt, Brace & World, 1955.

Luther, Martin. *Freedom of the Christian*.

Morris, Leon. *The Gospel According to St. Luke*. New Testament Commentaries. Grand Rapids, Mich.: Eerdmans, 1974.

Nicholas, Ron, et al. *Good Things Come in Small Groups*. Downers Grove, Ill.: InterVarsity Press, 1985.

Nicholas, Ron, et al. *Small Group Leaders' Handbook*. Downers Grove, Ill.: InterVarsity Press, 1981.

Nyquist, James, and Jack Kuhatschek. *Leading Bible Discussions*. Downers Grove: InterVarsity Press, 1985.

Nystrom, Carolyn. *Romans: Christianity on Trial*. Wheaton, Ill.: Harold Shaw, 1980.

Nystrom, Carolyn, and Matthew Floding. *Relationships: Face to Face*. Wheaton, Ill.: Harold Shaw, 1986.

Peterson, Eugene. *A Long Obedience in the Same Direction*. Downers Grove, Ill.: InterVarsity Press, 1980.

Plueddemann, Jim and Carol. *Pilgrims in Progress*. Wheaton: Harold Shaw, 1990.

Smith, Blaine. *Knowing God's Will*. Rev. ed. Downers Grove, Ill.: InterVarsity Press, 1991.

Tenney, Merrill C., gen. ed. *The Zondervan Pictoral Encyclopedia of the Bible*. Grand Rapids, Mich.: Zondervan, 1976.

Tyndale New Testament Commentaries. Grand Rapids, Mich.: Eerdmans.

Wesley, John and Charles. *Selected Prayers, Hymns, Journal Notes, Sermons, Letters and Treatises*. New York: Paulist Press, 1981.

White, John. *Magnificent Obsession*. Downers Grove, Ill.: InterVarsity Press, rev. 1990.

Christian Character Bible Studies from InterVarsity Press
in 6 or 12 studies for individuals or groups

Deciding Wisely by Bill Syrios. Making tough decisions is part of life. Through these Bible studies, you'll find out how to pray for God's will, listen to his voice and become a wise person. These principles of godly decision-making will enable you to serve God in the decisions you make. 1148-6.

Finding Contentment by Carolyn Nystrom. The contentment that character-izes the Christian life is found in intangibles—trust, love, joy, comfort and hope. The studies in this guide will introduce you to these keys to complete fulfillment in Christ. 1145-1.

Living in the World by Carolyn Nystrom. How do we glorify God in secular work? How should we spend our money? What kind of political involvement should we have? This guide is designed to help us clarify godly values so that we will not be affected by the warped values of the world. 1144-3.

Loving God by Carolyn Nystrom. Studies on how God loves—and how his gracious and stubborn love provide the foundation for our love for him. As we learn to love God as he loves us, we'll learn how to be more who he wants us to be. 1141-9.

Loving One Another by Carolyn Nystrom. This guide will help you to solve your differences with other Christians, learn to worship together, encourage one another and open up to each other. Discover the bond of love between believers that is a joyful tie! 1142-7.

Loving the World by Carolyn Nystrom. God has created a glorious world. Our responsibility is to help preserve and protect it. From valuing the sanctity of life to sharing your faith to helping the oppressed to protecting the envi-ronment, these Bible studies will help you discover your role in God's crea-tion. 1143-5.

Pursuing Holiness by Carolyn Nystrom. Character traits such as honesty, self-control, sexual purity and integrity may seem out of date. Yet, God's will for us is that we live holy lives. Through Christ, we can find the strength we need to live in a way that glorifies God. These studies will help you to pursue the traits of holiness. 1147-8.

Staying Faithful by Andrea Sterk Louthan and Howard Louthan. This study guide is about wholehearted commitment to Christ. We will be motivated not only to persevere in Christ, but also to grow by taking the risks that will allow us to move forward in our Christian lives. Discover the power of faithfulness! 1146-X.